CONTENTS

PREFACE

The aim of this book is to present in clear form the simple principles of investment, and to afford the reader a working knowledge of the various classes of securities which are available as investments and their relative adaptability to different needs. The book is an outgrowth of the writer's personal experience as an investment banker. Most of the matter which is presented has appeared in the pages of "System" Magazine, through the courtesy of whose editors it is now rearranged and consolidated for publication in book form.

G. G. H.

I

GENERAL PRINCIPLES OF INVESTMENT

With the immense increase in wealth in the United States during the last decade and its more general distribution, the problem of investment has assumed correspondingly greater importance. As long as the average business man was an habitual borrower of money and possest no private fortune outside of his interest in his business, he was not greatly concerned with investment problems. The surplus wealth of the country for a long time was in the hands of financial institutions and a few wealthy capitalists. These men, the officers and directors of banks, savings-banks, and insurance companies, and the possessors of hereditary wealth, were thoroughly equipped by training and experience for the solving of investment problems and needed no help in the disposition of the funds under their control. During the last ten years, however, these conditions have been greatly altered. The number of business men to-day in possession of funds in excess of their private wants and business requirements is far greater than it was ten years ago, and is constantly increasing. These men are confronted with a real investment problem.

While they have not always recognized it, the problem which they are called upon to solve is really twofold—it concerns the safeguarding of their private fortune and the wise disposition of their business surplus. They have usually seen the first part of this problem, but not all have succeeded in clearly understanding the second. When the treatment of a man's business surplus is spoken of as an investment problem, it is meant, of course, not his working capital, which should be kept in liquid form for immediate needs, but that portion of his surplus which is set aside for emergencies. It is coming to be a recognized principle that every business enterprise of whatever kind or size should establish a reserve fund. It is felt that the possession of a reserve fund puts the business upon a secure foundation, adds to its financial strength and reputation, and greatly increases its credit and borrowing capacity. The recognition of this fact, combined with the ability to set aside a reserve fund, has brought many men to a consideration of the best way in which to dispose of it. It is obviously a waste of income to have the surplus in bank-accounts; more than that, there would be a constant temptation to use it and to confuse it with working capital. Its best disposition is plainly in some safe interest-bearing security, which can be readily sold, so that it will be available for use if necessity demands.

Confronted with the double problem thus outlined, what measure of success has attended the average business man in its solution?

It is safe to say that the average man has found it easier to make money than to take care of it. Money-making, for him, is the result of successful activity in his own line of business, with which he is thoroughly familiar; while the investment of money is a thing apart from his business, with which he is not familiar, and of which he may have had little practical experience. His failure to invest money wisely is not due to any want of intelligence or of proper care and foresight on his part, as he sometimes seems to believe, but simply because he is ignorant of the principles of a business which differs radically from his own.

The investment of money is a banker's business. When the average man has funds to invest, whether he be a business man or a pure investor, he should consult some experienced and reliable investment banker just as he would consult a doctor or a lawyer if he were in need of medical or legal advice. This book is not intended to take the place of consultation with a banker, but to supplement it.

The advantage of such consultation is shown by the fact that if a man attempts to rely on his own judgment, he is almost certain not to do the best thing, even if his business instinct leads him to avoid those enterprises which are more plainly unpromising or fraudulent. It should be remembered, however, that widows and orphans are not the only ones ensnared by attractive advertisements and the promise of brilliant returns. In most cases, widows' and orphans' funds are protected by conscientious and conservative trustees, and it is the average business man who furnishes the money which is ultimately lost in all propositions which violate the fundamental laws of investment.

The average man is led into these unwise investments through a very natural error of judgment. Accustomed to take reasonable chances and to make large returns in his own business, he fails to detect anything fundamentally wrong in a proposition simply because it promises to pay well. He forgets that the rate of interest on *invested money*, or pure interest, is very small, and that anything above that can only come as payment for management, as he makes in his own business, or at the sacrifice of some essential factor of safety which will usually lead to disaster.

For the successful investment of money, however, a good deal more is required than the mere ability to select a safe security. That is only one phase of the problem. Scientific investment demands a clear understanding of the fundamental distinctions between different classes of securities and strict adherence to the two cardinal principles, distribution of risk and selection of securities in accordance with real requirements.

One of the most important distinctions is that between *promises to pay* and *equities*. Bonds, real-estate mortgages, and loans on collateral represent somebody's promise to pay a certain sum of money at a future date; and if the promise be good and the security ample, the holder of the promise will be paid the money at the time due. On the other hand, *equities*, such as the capital stocks of banking, railway, and industrial corporations, represent only a certain residuary share in the assets and profits of a working concern, after payment of its obligations and fixt charges. The value of this residuary share may be large or small, may increase or diminish, but in no case can the holder of such a share require any one, least of all the company itself, to redeem the certificate representing his interest at the price he paid for it, nor indeed at any price. If a man buys a $1,000 railroad bond, he knows that the railroad, if solvent, will pay him $1,000 in cash when the bond is due. But if he buys a share of railroad stock, his only chance of getting his money back, if he should wish it, is that some one else will want to buy his share for what he paid for it, or more. In one case he has bought a *promise to pay*, and in the other an *equity*.

It is not the intention, from the foregoing, to draw the conclusion that *equities* under no circumstances are to be regarded as investments, because many of our bank and railroad stocks, and even some of our public-utility and industrial stocks, have attained a stability and permanence of value and possess sufficiently long dividend records to justify their consideration when investments are contemplated; but it is essential that the investor should have a thorough understanding of the distinction involved.

The principle of distribution of risk is a simple one. It involves no more than obedience to the old rule which forbids putting all one's eggs in the same basket. The number of men who carry out this principle with any thoroughness, however, is very small. Proper distribution means not only the division of property among the various forms of investment, as railroad bonds, municipals, mortgages, public-utility bonds, etc., but also the preservation of proper geographical proportions within each form. Adherence to this principle is perhaps not so important for private investors as for institutions. A striking instance of the need for insistence upon its observance in the institutional field was furnished by one of the fire-insurance companies of San Francisco after the earthquake. It appeared that the company's assets were largely invested in San Francisco real estate and in local enterprises generally, where the bulk of its fire risks were concentrated. As a result, the very catastrophe which converted its risks into actual liabilities deprived its assets of all immediate value. This instance serves to show the importance of the principle and the necessity for its observance.

The principle of selection in accordance with real requirements is more complex. It involves a thorough understanding of the chief points which must be considered in the selection of all investments. These are five in number: (1) *Safety of principal and interest*, or the assurance of receiving the principal and interest on the dates due; (2) *rate of income*, or the net return which is realized on the actual amount of money invested; (3) *convertibility into cash*, or the readiness with which it is possible to realize on the investment; (4) *prospect of appreciation in value*, or that growth in intrinsic value which tends to advance market price; and (5) *stability of market price*, or the likelihood of maintaining the integrity of the principal invested.

The five qualities above enumerated are present in different degrees in every investment, and the scientific investor naturally selects those securities which possess in a high degree the qualities upon which he wishes to place emphasis. A large part of the problem of investment lies in the careful selection of securities to meet one's actual requirements. The average investor does not thoroughly understand this point. He does not realize that a high degree of one quality involves a lower degree of other qualities. He may have a general impression that a high rate of income is apt to indicate less assurance of safety, but he rarely applies the same reasoning to other qualities. When he buys securities, he is quite likely to pay for qualities which he does not need. It is very common, for example, when he wishes to make a permanent investment and has no thought of reselling, to find him purchasing securities which possess in a high degree the quality of convertibility. From his point of view, this is pure waste. A high degree of convertibility is only obtained at the sacrifice of some other quality—usually rate of income. If he were to use more care in his selections, he could probably find some other security possessing equal safety, equal stability, and equal promise of appreciation in value, which would yield considerably greater revenue, lacking only ready convertibility. Thus he would satisfy his real requirements and obtain a greater income, at the expense only of a quality which he does not need.

The quality of convertibility divides investors into classes more sharply than any other quality. For some investors convertibility is a matter of small importance; for others it is the paramount consideration. Generally speaking, the private investor does not need to place much emphasis upon the quality of convertibility, at least for the larger part of his estate. On the other hand, for a business surplus, ready convertibility is an absolute necessity, and in order to secure it, something in the way of income must usually be sacrificed.

Again, some investors are so situated that they can insist strongly upon promise of appreciation in value, while others can not afford to do so. Rich men whose income is in excess of their wants, can afford to forego something in the way of yearly return for the sake of a strong prospect of appreciation in value. Such men naturally buy bank and trust-company stocks, whose general characteristic is a small return upon the money invested, but a strong likelihood of appreciation in value. This is owing to the general practise of well-regulated banks to distribute only about half their earnings in dividends and to credit the rest to surplus, thus insuring a steady rise in the book value of the stock. Rich men, again, can afford to take chances with the quality of safety, for the sake of greater income, in a way which poor men should never do. In practise, however, if the writer's observation can be depended upon, it is usually the poor men who take the chances—and lose their money.

In the quality of safety, there is a marked difference between safety of principal and safety of interest. With some investments the principal is much safer than the interest, and *vice versa*. This can best be illustrated by examples. The bonds of terminal companies, which are guaranteed as to interest, under the terms of a lease, by the railroads which use the terminal, are usually far safer as to interest than as to principal. While the lease lasts, the interest is probably perfectly secure, but when the lease expires and the bonds mature, the railroads may see fit to abandon the terminal and build one elsewhere, if the city has grown in another direction, and the terminal may cease to have any value except as real estate. On the other hand, a new railroad, built in a thinly settled but rapidly growing part of the country, may have difficulty in bad years in meeting its interest charges, and may even go into temporary default, but if the bonds are issued at a low rate per mile and the management of the road is honest and capable, the safety of the principal can scarcely be questioned.

Stability of market price is frequently a consideration of great importance. This quality should never be confused with the quality of safety. Safety means the assurance that the maker of the obligation will pay principal and interest when due; stability of market price means that the investment shall not shrink in quoted value. These are very different things, tho frequently identified in people's minds. An investment may possess assured safety of principal and interest and yet suffer a violent decline in quoted price, owing to a change in general business and financial conditions. In times of continued business prosperity very high rates are demanded for the use of money, because the liquid capital of the country, to a large extent, has been converted into fixt forms, in the development of new mines, the building of new factories and railroads, and in the improvement and extension of existing properties. These high rates have the effect of reducing the price level of investment securities because people having such securities are apt to sell them in order to lend the money so released, thus maintaining the parity between the yields upon free and invested capital.

As an illustration of this tendency, within the last few years New York City 3½-per-cent bonds have declined from 110 to 90, without the slightest suspicion of their safety. Their inherent qualities have changed in no respect except that their prospect of appreciation in quoted price has become decidedly brighter. Their fall in price has been due to two factors, one general and the other special—first, the absorption of liquid capital and consequent rise in interest rates, occasioned by the unprecedented business activity of the country, and, second, to the unfavorable technical position of the bonds, due to an increased supply in the face of a decreased demand.

It will be seen that the question of maintaining the integrity of the money invested is a matter of great importance and deserves to rank as a fifth factor in determining the selection of investments, altho it is not an inherent quality of each investment, but is dependent for its effect upon general conditions. If it is essential to the investor that his security should not shrink in quoted price, his best investment is a real-estate mortgage, which is not quoted and consequently does not fluctate. For the investment of a business surplus, however, where a high degree of convertibility is required, real-estate mortgages will not answer, and the best way to guard against shrinkage is to purchase a short-term security, whose approach to maturity will maintain the price close to par.

The foregoing comments, in a brief and imperfect way, serve to indicate the main points which should be considered in the selection of securities for investment. The considerations advanced will be amplified as occasion demands in the following pages. For the present, the main lesson which it is sought to draw is the necessity that a man should have a thorough understanding of his real requirements before he attempts to make investments. For a private investor to go to a banker and ask him to suggest a security to him without telling him the exact nature of his wants is about as foolish as it would be for a patient to go to a physician and ask him to give him some medicine without telling him the symptoms of the trouble which he wished cured. In neither case can the adviser act intelligently unless he knows what end he is seeking to accomplish.

It is plainly impossible within the limits of a small volume to consider the needs of all classes of investors. Special attention will be paid to the requirements of a business surplus and of the private investor. In the field of private investment two distinct classes can be recognized—those who are dependent upon income from investments and those who are not. Both classes will be considered. For the investment of a business surplus, safety, convertibility, and stability of price are the qualities to be emphasized; for investors dependent upon income, safety and a high return; and for those not dependent upon income, a high return and prospect of appreciation in value. In the following chapters railroad bonds, real-estate mortgages, industrial, public-utility, and municipal bonds and stocks will be considered in turn; their advantages and disadvantages will be analyzed in accordance with the determining qualities above enumerated, and their adaptability to the requirements of a business surplus and of private investment will be discust.

II

RAILROAD MORTGAGE BONDS

A railroad bond is an obligation of a railroad company (usually secured by mortgage upon railroad property) which runs for a certain length of time at a certain rate of interest. It is apparent, from this definition, that the price of a railroad bond, as distinct from its value, is affected by two *accidental conditions* quite apart from the five determining qualities described in the preceding chapter.

These accidental conditions are the length of time that the bond has to run and the rate of interest that it bears. To understand clearly the influence of these accidental conditions is a matter of the utmost importance. It is evident, for instance, that a 5-per-cent fifty-year bond, based on a given security, will sell at a widely different price from a 3½-per-cent twenty-year bond, based on the same security; yet the only difference is in the accidental conditions which are under the control of the board of directors.

In order to eliminate these accidental features from the situation, it is customary for bond-dealers to classify bonds purely on the basis of their yield, or net income return. As a thorough understanding of this point is essential to an accurate judgment of bond values, whether railroad bonds or otherwise, it must be developed in detail, even at the risk of carrying the reader over familiar ground.

If a bond sells above par, it does not yield its purchaser a net return as great as the rate of interest which the bond bears, for two reasons: first, because the loss in principal, represented by the premium which the purchaser pays, must be distributed over the number of years which the bond has to run, and operates to reduce the rate of interest which the holder receives; and, secondly, because the rate is paid only on the par value of the bond instead of on the actual money invested. Thus, if a 6-percent bond with eight years to run sells at 110¾, it will yield only 4.40 per cent, which means that if the holder spends more than $48.73 (4.40 per cent of $1,107.50) out of the $60 which he receives annually, he is spending the excess out of principal, and not out of income. Conversely, if a bond sells below par, it yields more than the rate of interest which the bond bears.

These yields have been calculated with the utmost exactness for all bonds paying from 2 per cent to 7 per cent and running from six months to one hundred years, so that it is only necessary to turn to the tables to discover what will be the net return upon a given bond at a given price. This net return is generally known as the "basis," and bonds are spoken of as selling upon a 3.80 per cent basis or a 4.65 per cent basis or whatever the figure may be, with no reference whatever to the price or to the rate of interest which the bond bears. Indeed, so exclusively is the basis considered by bond-dealers that very often bonds are bought and sold upon a basis price, and the actual figures at which the bonds change hands are not determined until after the transaction is concluded.

It is not expected, of course, that the average business man will purchase bonds in quite as scientific a way as this, but it is essential that he should understand that while the intrinsic value of a bond is determined only by the five general factors described, its money value, or price, is affected also by these two accidental conditions. Exprest in other words, he must realize that the general factor described as *rate of income* does not mean the coupon rate of interest which the bond bears, but the scientific "basis," derived by elimination of the accidental features.

Within the past year there has been a good deal of uninformed comment about the safety of railroad bonds. Before the era of popular agitation and governmental antagonism, railroad bonds enjoyed a large measure of public confidence; but it can not be denied that some part of this confidence has been shaken as a result of the recent exposures. Even clearheaded men have exaggerated the importance of the developments; and too often railroad officials, who should have insisted upon the soundness and stability of their properties, when they elected to talk for publication, have given way instead to dismal and unwarranted forebodings.

There is no mystery involved in determining the safety of railroad bonds. Any man of business experience, keeping in mind the general principle which measures the value of all obligations, can easily determine, with the aid of two documents, the degree of safety which attaches to any particular railroad bond. The general principle to be observed is that the safety of any obligation depends upon the margin of security in excess of the amount of the loan; and the two documents to be consulted are the mortgage or trust indenture securing the bonds, which describes the property mortgaged, and the last annual report of the railroad, which shows its financial condition.

Confining the analysis, for the present, to mortgage bonds upon the general mileage of a railroad, the following points should be considered:

(1) *Rate per mile at which the bond is issued.* Applying the general principle indicated above, it must be learned what proportion the bonded debt of a railroad bears to the total market value of the property. It is much easier to make this comparison on a per-mile basis. In determining whether the rate per mile is excessive, reference must be made not so much to the particular bond in question as to the total bonded debt per mile of the railroad, and to the relation which that figure bears to the total market value of the property per mile. The total market value per mile is obtained by adding the market value of the stock per mile to the par value of the bonded debt per mile. A single issue of bonds varies all the way from $5,000 to $100,000 per mile, according to the location of the railroad. Total capitalization per mile—stocks and bonds at par—varies in about the same proportion, from $35,000 to $300,000. The average for all the railroads of the United States is $67,936 per mile. The actual cost of the railroad, as shown by the balance-sheet, must be taken into consideration, and also the estimated cost of duplicating the property. Physical difficulties of construction must be weighed, for a railroad through a flat, sandy country should not be bonded for as much, other things being equal, as a railroad through a mountainous country, where much cutting, filling, and bridging are required. The section of country in which the railroad is located must be considered, for $35,000 per mile on a single-track line in a poor country may be higher than $300,000 per mile on a four-track trunk line which owns valuable terminals and rights of way through several large cities.

(2) *Amount of prior lien bonds outstanding per mile.* The amount of bonds which come ahead of the bond in question on the same mileage is a matter of great importance and works directly against the security of the bond. Purchasing a bond which is preceded by a prior line bond is like taking a

real-estate mortgage on property already encumbered. If the bond is not followed by other bonds, then the margin of security in the property is represented wholly by the market value of the stock per mile, and the investor must figure carefully the value of this equity.

(3) *Amount of junior lien bonds outstanding per mile.* The amount of bonds which come after the bond in question, on the other hand, works directly in favor of the bond, for it increases the margin of security. It shows also that other people have had sufficient confidence in the property to invest their money in obligations subject to the one in question. In the event of a receivership this is often a matter of great importance; for if a foreclosure sale is ordered the junior bondholders, in order to protect their own interest, must buy in the property for an amount at least equal to the par value of the prior lien bonds.

The foregoing considerations apply particularly to the safety of the principal invested in railroad bonds; the following points affect the safety of interest:

(4) *Gross earnings per mile.* The gross earnings of a railroad must be compared with those of other roads occupying the same field, and the returns for a number of years must be examined to determine whether such earnings have increased or decreased. The position in which the railroad stands for obtaining new traffic must be noted. This is dependent somewhat upon the railroad's ability to take traffic from other railroads, but more upon the probable growth and development of the territory which the railroad serves, and the increased traffic which will probably be offered. In this connection the rate of increase in population in the road's territory is important. The proportion between passenger and freight earnings, the diversity and density of freight traffic, and passenger and freight rates should be examined. The reputation of the management for ability and integrity should be considered. Gross earnings run from about $3,000 to $40,000 per mile with the average $10,460.

(5) *Net income per mile.* Net income is obtained by subtracting from gross earnings operating expenses (and sometimes taxes) and adding to the net earnings so obtained whatever income from other sources the railroad may derive. This is a very important figure. As with gross earnings, the reports

should be examined to determine whether net income is on the increase or the decrease, and it should be compared with the net income of other railroads occupying the same field. It involves a criticism of operating expenses. The payments of the railroad must be analyzed to determine whether the proper sums have been expended for maintenance of way, replenishment of rolling stock, and other improvements sufficient to keep the road in good physical condition. Normally speaking, operating expenses should absorb about 65 per cent of gross earnings. If it is found that a railroad operates for 60 per cent, however, it does not always follow that its operating officials are exceptionally efficient, so that the cost of conducting transportation is relatively small; it may mean that the physical condition of the property is being neglected, or that ordinary improvements, which should be charged to maintenance, are being paid for by increase in capitalization. It is very important for the investor to find out which is the case. If analysis leads to the suspicion that the earnings result from neglecting the property or capitalizing every trivial improvement, the railroad's bonds should be rejected. Net income varies from $1,500 to $12,000 per mile, with an average of $4,702.

(6) *Fixt charges per mile.* The fixt charges of a railroad include interest on its bonds, rentals, and taxes (when the last-named are not reported with operating expenses). The importance of this figure lies in its relation to net income. If a railroad does not earn well over double its fixt charges, its obligations can not be regarded as in the first investment rank. Of course, when a railroad earns more than twice the interest requirement upon its entire bonded debt, it is probable that some of the underlying bonds are protected by three, four, or five times the interest requirement upon them, and their position is correspondingly strengthened.

The foregoing analysis applies particularly to mortgage bonds upon the general mileage of a railroad and not to such special issues as collateral trust, terminal, bridge, or guaranteed bonds. It will not be necessary, however, to lay down any rules as to these classes of bonds, for the general principles outlined above, with slight modifications of detail, will be found equally applicable to a judgment of their value. Equipment bonds, on the other hand, owing to their want of similarity to any other railroad issues, will receive separate treatment later.

It is of interest, in view of the present diminished confidence in railroad securities, to advance certain considerations touching upon the safety of railroad bonds in general.

The last published report of the Inter-State Commerce Commission, year 1906, furnishes interesting testimony on this subject. A table on page 60 shows that the total railroad capital of the United States for that year was $14,570,421,478, of which $7,766,661,385, or 53.31 per cent, was in the form of bonded debt, and the rest in capital stock.

These figures indicate a substantial equity, but are somewhat misleading because they refer to par value. A fair estimate of the market value of this stock equity, which is the margin of security in the properties from the bondholder's point of view, can be obtained from a table on page 82, which shows a balance available for dividends, after paying all operating expenses and fixt charges, of all the railroads of the United States for the year ended June 30, 1906, of $457,060,326. This amount is equivalent to nearly 7 per cent upon the total par value of the stocks.

Estimating that a railroad stock should earn 10 per cent upon its market price—and even the most prejudiced will admit that a stock earning 10 per cent is worth par—the total market value of American railroad stocks would be $4,570,603,260, or more than half the par value of the bonds. In other words, the bonded debt would represent something less than 63 per cent of the total market value of the property. This compares favorably with the security of first mortgages upon real estate.

When the safety of interest is considered, the showing made is equally strong. Page 82 of the report above quoted shows that the net income of the railroads of the United States for the year ended June 30, 1906, after payment of all operating expenses, was $848,836,771, and the total fixt charges, including interest on bonds, interest on current liabilities, and taxes, amounted to $391,776,445, leaving a balance available for dividends of $457,060,326. It is apparent, therefore, that the net earnings of the railroads of the United States, considered as one system, could be cut in half without affecting the payment of interest upon the railroad's obligations. This affords a large measure of protection.

The following analysis shows that the actual market value of the railroads is probably greater than the estimate made above.

The table shows the percentage of bonded debt to total market value of some of the more important railroad systems. Two trunk lines in the East, a north and south line in the middle West, and two transcontinental have been chosen. No attempt has been made to select railroads which would make a favorable showing. Indeed Pennsylvania, and Union Pacific, by reason of their recent heavy bond issues, probably compare unfavorably with others which might have been chosen. The figures showing the par value of bonds outstanding have been taken from last annual reports, with additions made for recent issues. The figures showing the market value of stocks are based on the amounts outstanding April 1st, 1908, at the market price.

	Par value of bonds outstanding	Approx. market value of stock outstanding	Per cent of bonds to total value
Pennsylvania	$270,974,645	$361,000,000	42.8
New York Central	255,414,845	174,000,000	59.4
Illinois Central	156,053,275	120,000,000	56.6
Great Northern	207,517,939	260,000,000	44.3
Union Pacific	274,827,000	324,000,000	45.9

In view of the enormous decline which has occurred in railroad stocks during the past eighteen months, the showing above is truly remarkable. It is plain that the entire bonded debt of any of these standard railroads is less than 60 per cent of the total market value of the property, while in the cases of the Pennsylvania, Great Northern, and Union Pacific, *more than half of the present market value of the property could be erased before the lien of the bonds least well secured would be impaired.*

Of course, where the entire bonded debt is protected by such a margin, it is evident that the underlying bonds (the prior liens and first mortgages) are protected by several times as great a margin and their position is correspondingly strengthened.

The foregoing analysis, in the judgment of the writer, affords convincing proof not only that the prevailing want of confidence in railroad obligations is without foundation, but that railroad bonds compare favorably in point of safety with any other form of investment.

It remains to point out the amount of income and degree of convertibility which they afford and the extent of appreciation in value which they promise. It is impossible to do more than indicate the general characteristics of railroad bonds in these particulars.

Railroad bonds cover a wide range of income return. They yield all the way from 3¾ per cent to 9 per cent, the general average being from 4 per cent to 6 per cent. As a class they yield more than government or municipal bonds, and less than public-utility or industrial bonds. With equal security they probably yield less than real-estate mortgages. Compared with stocks they return more than bank stocks, average about the same as railroad stocks, and yield less than public-utility, industrial, or mining stocks. These comparisons are intended to apply to the classes as a whole, and remain generally true in spite of specific cases to the contrary.

Convertibility is the distinguishing mark of railroad bonds. Generally speaking they may be more easily marketed than any other class of bonds. Compared with stocks they exceed public-utility, mining, and bank stocks in point of convertibility, and yield only to railroad stocks. It is hard to say whether or not they possess greater convertibility than industrial stocks, but it is probable that they do, allowing for the fact that an undue impression is created by the activity of certain prominent shares.

Railroad bonds as a class possess great promise of appreciation in value. American railroads, generally speaking, have adopted the conservative policy of putting a considerable part of their annual earnings back into the property in the form of improvements. To the extent to which this policy is followed, an equity is created back of the bonds which raises their intrinsic value. This policy contrasts favorably with the general practise of English roads to pay out all their earnings in dividends, and to capitalize their improvements. In addition, new capital for American railroads is largely raised by stock issues, which further increases the margin of security for the bondholders. Taken together these facts insure a steady enhancement in the intrinsic value of railroad bonds, which is bound to be reflected, other things being equal, in higher prices.

We shall not attempt to discuss at this time the degree of stability of market price which railroad bonds enjoy. As explained in the first chapter, stability of market price is dependent upon general financial and business conditions. It is sufficient to point out here that the maintenance intact of the principal sum invested can only be rendered certain by the purchase of short-time securities whose near approach to maturity will keep their price close to par. In a later chapter the general principles which determine this question will be elucidated.

The ideal investment may be defined as one combining ample security of principal and interest, a good rate of income, ready convertibility into cash, and reasonable promise of appreciation in value. Measured by the requirements of this definition, the conclusion seems justified that well-selected railroad bonds, if purchased under favorable money-market conditions, afford a highly desirable form of investment.

III

RAILROAD EQUIPMENT BONDS

As its name implies, an equipment bond is one issued by a railroad to provide funds with which to pay for new rolling stock—cars and locomotives. The issues are variously described as car trust certificates, equipment bonds, or equipment notes. They conform in general to one of two standard forms: (1) The conditional sale plan: In accordance with specifications furnished by the railroad, the trustee selected (usually a trust company) contracts with the builders for the purchase of the equipment. From 10 to 20 per cent of the cost of the equipment is paid in cash by the railroad and the rest is represented by the equipment bonds. The bonds are the direct obligation of the railroad company. They are secured by a first lien upon the entire equipment purchased. The title to the equipment remains in the trustee for the benefit of the bondholders until the last bond has been paid, so that under no circumstances can the general mortgages of the railroad attach as a first lien on the equipment ahead of the car trust obligations. After the final payment, the trustee assigns title to the railroad company, which thereupon becomes the owner in fee of the equipment. Under the terms of the deed of trust the railroad is always obliged to keep the equipment fully insured, in good order and complete repair, and to replace any equipment which may become worn out, lost, or destroyed. The bonds are usually issued in coupon form, $1,000 each, bearing semiannual interest, with provision for registration. They are generally paid off in semiannual or annual instalments of substantially equal amounts, the last instalment usually falling due in ten years, a period well within the life of the equipment as estimated under the master car builder's rules. Occasionally this method of payment is altered by the substitution of a sinking fund, the bonds having a uniform fixt maturity, but subject to the operation of a sinking fund which is sufficient to retire the entire issue well within the life of the equipment. In either case the security, ample at the outset, increases proportionally with the reduction in obligations outstanding against it.

(2) The so-called "Philadelphia plan." Under this plan the equipment is purchased by an individual, association, or corporation which leases the equipment to the railroad for a term of years at a rental equivalent to the interest and maturing instalments of the bonds. The contract of lease is then assigned to a trust company as trustee, which thereupon issues its certificates in substantially the form described in the plan above, these representing a beneficial interest in the equipment, which are usually guaranteed both principal and interest by the railroad. The lease runs until the last bond has been paid, after which the trustee assigns title to the railroad as above. The chief advantage of this plan over the other is that in some States, notably Pennsylvania, certificates issued in accordance with its terms are exempt from taxation, whereas under the conditional sale plan, as the direct obligation of the railroad, the bonds would be taxable.

It is evident from the foregoing description that equipment bonds differ in two important respects from all other classes of railroad issues. First, the title to the property which secures the bonds does not vest in the railroad; and, secondly, the property is movable and not fixt in any one locality.

By virtue of these two points, the holders of equipment bonds possess a great advantage over the holders of mortgage bonds in the event of a railroad's becoming bankrupt.

If a railroad is unable to meet its interest charges, the mortgage bondholders can rarely do better than have a receiver appointed who will operate the railroad in their interest; but if, with honest and efficient management, the railroad can not be made to earn its interest charges, the mortgage bondholders usually have to consent to the scaling of their bonds to a point where the railroad can operate upon a paying basis.

With the holders of equipment bonds the case is quite different. If the receiver defaults upon their bonds they have only to direct the trustee to enter upon possession of the equipment and sell it or lease it to some other railroad. The knowledge that they possess this power renders its exercise generally unnecessary. The equipment of a railroad is essential to its operation. It is the tool with which the railroad handles its business. If the receiver were deprived of the equipment it would be impossible for him to operate the road, and so he could never satisfy its creditors. Consequently the courts, both State and Federal, have ruled that the necessary equipment of a bankrupt railroad must be preserved, and have placed the charges for principal and interest of equipment obligations upon an equality with charges for wages, materials, and other operating expenses, and in priority to interest of even first-mortgage bonds.

These points sufficiently explain the remarkable record which equipment bonds have made during reorganizations. Careful investigation has been made of the various railroads which were reorganized, either with or without foreclosure, between the years 1888 and 1905. This covers the chief period of railroad receivership. It was discovered that sixteen different railroads, aggregating nearly one hundred thousand miles and located in widely different parts of the country, had outstanding equipment bonds at the time of default. In every case the principal and interest of equipment bonds were paid in full, while all other securities, with a few exceptions, were reduced in rate or amount or both. Two of these railroads offered to the holders of equipment bonds the option of an advantageous exchange of securities, which amounted to more than payment in full.

The foregoing facts justify the conclusion that equipment bonds possess security equal or superior to that of any other form of railroad bonds.

Let us now consider their remaining characteristics—their rate of income, convertibility, prospect of appreciation in value, and stability of market price.

One of the strongest features of equipment bonds is the relatively high rate of income which they yield. The amount realized varies in accordance with the financial strength and credit of the issuing railroad, and the margin of security in the equipment itself. As a general rule, the net return on the equipment bonds of a given railroad is usually from ½ per cent to ¾ per cent greater than on the first-mortgage bonds of the same railroad. This is owing to the fact that while banks and scientific investors have bought equipment bonds for many years, the general public is not sufficiently familiar with the inherent strength of these issues to create much of a demand for them. This insures a good return.

Equipment bonds vary in point of convertibility. The reader will remember from the description above that equipment bonds are usually issued in serial form, with instalments maturing semiannually from six months to ten years. By confining purchases to the shorter maturities, say within two or three years, a high degree of convertibility may usually be obtained because the short maturities are greatly sought by banks and other financial institutions which regard equipment bonds in much the same light as merchant's paper or time loans secured by collateral. At a price equivalent to the rate which the best commercial paper commands, there is always a good demand from the banks. Many banks prefer equipment bonds to loans or paper on account of their greater convertibility. As the length of maturity increases, the degree of convertibility generally decreases, because the chief demand for the longer dates comes from insurance companies, which do not, in the aggregate, constitute as great a demand as the banks. When the demand from private investors increases, as it undoubtedly will when they become more familiar with the desirable points of these issues, all maturities will probably possess ready convertibility.

In the same way, equipment bonds vary as to stability of market price. Compared with other classes of railroad issues, equipment bonds are all relatively stable, but the stability is especially marked in the shorter maturities.

Equipment bonds possess little prospect of appreciation in value.

The attentive reader who has carefully followed the foregoing description of equipment bonds, may have noticed a special adaptability on their part to the requirements of a business surplus. Broadly speaking, for such investment, a security is required which will combine perfect safety of principal and interest, a good rate of income, ready convertibility into cash, and unyielding stability of market price. The necessity for insistence upon these requirements in the investment of a business surplus will appear upon a moment's reflection. Safety is required in all forms of investment, but is particularly important in the handling of business funds; a good rate of income is always desirable; convertibility is necessary for a business surplus so that the reserve funds may be converted into cash at any time; and it is of the utmost importance that the security should not shrink materially in quoted price, no matter what changes may take place in financial and business conditions, so that if the need should arise for realizing on the reserve fund, it would be found unimpaired in amount. As explained in a former chapter, this point can not be covered by the selection of securities perfectly safe as to principal and interest, but only by the purchase of short-term obligations.

The point may be illustrated as follows: Let it be supposed that a firm or company has decided to invest $100,000 in the 5-per-cent equipment bonds of a good railroad maturing in three years, which can be obtained at par, merchant's paper then commanding about 5½ per cent. After two years it becomes necessary for the firm to realize on its investment at a time when commercial paper is floated with difficulty on a 6½-per-cent or 7-per-cent basis. Under such money conditions the equipment bonds could be sold on about a 6-per-cent basis, which would mean a price of 99 for a 5-per-cent bond with one year to run. The firm, in liquidating its investment, would therefore lose 1 per cent in principal, but would have received 5 per cent interest for two years, making the net return 4½ per cent. Compare this showing with the result if the bonds when originally bought had had ten years to run instead of three.

After two years, when the firm wished to dispose of its bonds it might experience some difficulty in doing so in the stringent money market which has been supposed, but even if it succeeded in selling them upon a 6-per-cent basis, that would mean a price of only 93¾ and would represent 6¼-per-cent loss in principal. If it were necessary to sell the bonds upon a higher basis or if the firm had purchased a bond with more than ten years to run, the relative disadvantage of the longer bond would be still more apparent. These points sufficiently demonstrate the importance of buying only short-term securities for the investment of a business surplus. Of course, if money conditions improve instead of becoming worse between the dates of purchase and sale, then a greater profit would be made with the longer-term bond. This, however, should not be allowed to influence the choice, first because it is not the object of a reserve fund to make a speculative profit, and secondly because a firm or corporation is only likely to want to realize upon its reserve fund when money is hard to obtain otherwise, and that is precisely the time when any long-term bond would be apt to show considerable depreciation.

The foregoing considerations indicate a special adaptability on the part of equipment bonds to the usual requirements of a business surplus. The points have been brought out at some length because of the importance of the subject to the average business man. The purpose in concentrating attention upon a single instance has been to illustrate more clearly the principles involved and at the same time to acquaint the business man with details of a highly desirable and somewhat unfamiliar form of security.

IV

REAL-ESTATE MORTGAGES

In the preceding chapter the discussion of railroad bonds was brought to a close. Before passing to the consideration of real-estate mortgages, which is the next form of investment to be taken up, it may be well to review briefly the general principles advanced in the first chapter of this book, in order that the reader may have clearly in mind the main points upon which judgment of the value of investments should be based.

There are five chief points to be considered in the selection of all forms of investment. These are: (1) safety of principal and interest; (2) rate of income; (3) convertibility into cash; (4) prospect of appreciation in intrinsic value; (5) stability of market price.

Keeping these five general factors in mind, the present chapter will discuss real-estate mortgages as a form of investment, both as adapted to the requirements of private funds and of a business surplus.

The average American business man is so familiar with real-estate mortgages that the details may be passed over briefly. A real-estate mortgage, or a bond and mortgage, as it is sometimes called, consists essentially of two parts, a bond or promise to pay a certain sum of money at a future date with interest at a certain rate per annum, and a mortgage or trust deed transferring title and ownership in a piece of real estate, with the provision that the transfer shall be void if the interest is regularly paid and the bond redeemed at maturity. Before advancing money on the security of a mortgage it is necessary to determine whether the title to the property legally vests in the maker of the mortgage; and during the continuance of the mortgage it is necessary to have proof that the taxes and assessments are being regularly paid, and, in the case of improved property, the fire-insurance as well.

The safety of real-estate mortgages, in common with the safety of all obligations, depends upon the margin of security in excess of the amount of the loan. In the case of real-estate mortgages the amount of this margin may be determined without great difficulty. It is only necessary to have the property carefully appraised by an expert in real-estate values. It does not follow, however, because a mortgage has been shown to possess substantial equity, that it is perfectly safe as an investment, unless it satisfies also another condition of great importance. A mortgage may not exceed 50 per cent of the selling value of the real estate pledged, and yet be a poor investment. This point involves a serious objection to real-estate mortgages which sometimes escapes notice.

The holder of a mortgage is at a great disadvantage in regard to the changing value of real estate. If the value of the property upon which he holds a mortgage increases, the additional value enhances the security of the loan, but does not add to the principal which he has invested, while if the value of the property diminishes, not only is the security proportionately lessened, but if the impairment be great, the holder is frequently compelled to take over the property and may suffer loss of principal. In other words, he receives no direct benefit from an increase in the value of the property, but has to stand the larger part of the risk of a decline in its value.

This is not the case with investments represented by negotiable securities subject to changing market quotations. All such securities, railroad bonds for example, are acted on equally by changes in the value of the property which secures them. Except for the influences of money-market conditions, railroad bonds advance with an increase in the value of the property and decline with a decrease in its value. Well-selected bonds usually increase in value with time, and all such increase goes directly to the benefit of the holder. The failure of real-estate mortgages to respond similarly to changes in the value of property places the holder of a mortgage at a great disadvantage.

Owing to this characteristic, real-estate mortgages should be purchased only when general conditions in the real-estate market are distinctly favorable. Not only should the purchaser of a mortgage have sufficient margin of security in the particular piece of property upon which he is loaning money, but he should also be satisfied that general real-estate values are relatively low, that there has been no undue speculation, and that conditions favor an advance rather than a decline in real-estate prices.

No class of property is subject to more rapid changes in value than real estate. After an extensive advance the holder of a mortgage may be insufficiently protected by the equity in the property, even if his mortgage represents only 60 per cent of the current appraised value of the real estate pledged. It may be that the 60 per cent which he has loaned represents the total value or more than the total value a few years before. When a rapid advance in values occurs, tho it may be largely justified by the growth and development of the territory, there is sure to be present an element of speculation which is likely to carry prices beyond the point of reason. When the turn comes and a severe collapse takes place, its effects are extremely disastrous, because, unlike speculation in stocks or commodities, no short selling exists in real estate to temper the fall, and the immobile form of capital makes liquidation impossible. These considerations serve to show the need for great prudence in the purchase of real-estate mortgages. If the investor exercises due care in these particulars, he is reasonably sure of obtaining a very high-grade security; if he neglects these precautions, he may suffer severe loss of principal.

No general figures are available which would indicate the degree of certainty attaching to the payment of interest upon real-estate mortgages. Certain classes of mortgages, such as those secured by unimproved real estate or dwellings, afford no direct security of interest payment other than the threat of foreclosure. Other classes, such as mortgages upon stores, hotels, or office-buildings, are often protected by a large income from the direct operation of the mortgaged premises, thus furnishing a security for the annual interest payment. The margin of protection in these cases varies greatly, so that no general conclusion can be drawn.

The other characteristics of real-estate mortgages may be passed over more briefly. It is generally conceded that mortgages return a higher rate of income than can be obtained upon any other form of investment which affords equal security. This constitutes their chief advantage.

Their chief disadvantage, on the other hand, lies in their entire want of convertibility. There is no market for real-estate mortgages, and except in special instances they can not be readily sold. The fact that they are not subject to quotation prevents them also from holding out any prospect of appreciation in value. Their very deficiency in this respect, however, constitutes an important advantage from another point of view. Since they are not quoted they can not shrink in market price in obedience to changes in financial and business conditions. The buyer of a mortgage is assured that he can carry his mortgage at par through periods when it may be necessary to mark down all negotiable securities subject to changing market quotations. This is frequently a matter of great importance.

The general characteristics of real-estate mortgages may be summarized as follows: (1) When carefully selected and purchased under favorable conditions, great safety of principal and interest; (2) a relatively high return; (3) a low degree of convertibility; (4) no prospect of appreciation in value; and (5) the practical certainty of maintaining the integrity of the principal invested.

Is a security possessing these characteristics a suitable investment for a business surplus? Only to a limited extent. The safety, high return, and assurance against loss in quoted value of principal are all highly desirable qualities for this purpose, but the lack of convertibility is a fatal defect. No consideration is of greater importance in the investment of a business surplus than a high degree of convertibility, so that if the need should arise the investment may be instantly liquidated. The fact that real-estate mortgages can not be readily disposed of makes it practically impossible to employ them for the investment of a business surplus.

Where convertibility is not an essential requirement, and where the want of promise of appreciation in value is not a serious matter, mortgages afford a very desirable form of investment. The characteristics which they possess in an eminent degree—safety, high return, and assurance against loss in quoted value of principal—are exactly suited to the ordinary requirements of savings-banks. Generally speaking, only a small proportion of a savings-bank's assets need be kept in liquid form or readily convertible, and accordingly they find mortgages highly desirable.

For the purpose of private investment the attractiveness of mortgages is not so easy to determine. Ordinarily, fluctuations in quoted values are of no great importance to the private investor, so that the absence of quotation which mortgages enjoy is not especially valuable. Their safety and high return are attractive qualities, but their want of convertibility and of prospect of appreciation in value are drawbacks. On the whole, the private investor may probably employ with advantage a certain part, but not too much of his estate in mortgage investments.

As part of a scientific and comprehensive scheme of investment, the special advantages of real-estate mortgages appear most prominently in the years following a business depression. During such a period real-estate values are usually relatively low, but beginning to advance, so that mortgages present their maximum margin of security. At such a time they compare most favorably with bonds and other investment securities which are subject to changing quotations, because such securities are then apt to be at their highest point under the combined influence of restored confidence and the low money rates which usually prevail. After several years of continued and increasing business prosperity the positions are just reversed.

No discussion of real-estate mortgages would be complete without allusion to the guaranteed mortgages which have been placed upon the market in great quantities within the past few years. Guaranteed mortgages are real-estate mortgages guaranteed as to principal and interest by substantial companies having large capital and surplus. In addition to the guaranty, the companies usually search and guarantee the title, see to it that the taxes, assessments, and insurance are paid, and perform the other services of a real-estate broker. Their compensation varies somewhat, but probably averages ½ per cent—that is, for example, they loan at 5 per cent and sell guaranteed mortgages to the investor at 4½.

The value of the guaranty may be considered from two points of view—first, in the event of a general decline in real-estate values, and, secondly, when a fall occurs in a particular piece of property or in a particular locality.

If a severe decline in real-estate values takes place, affecting all localities, it might become necessary for the holders of guaranteed mortgages to test the value of their guaranties. In such a case the question would arise how far the capital and surplus of the guaranteeing companies would extend in liquidating the mortgages which they had guaranteed. This would depend entirely upon the proportion between the capital and surplus of the companies and the total amount of outstanding mortgages guaranteed. Ordinarily the capital and surplus do not exceed 5 per cent of the mortgages, so that the average guaranty is good for about 5 per cent additional equity. On a piece of property worth $100,000, upon which a guaranteed mortgage of $60,000 exists, the guaranty would be worth $3,000, and would margin the property down to $57,000. This additional equity is of little value. It is probably unlikely that a 40-per-cent depreciation in value will take place, but the guaranty is not needed unless it does, and if it should occur, the depreciation is quite as likely to go to 50 per cent or more as to stop at 43.

From the second point of view the value of the guaranty is much greater. The distribution of risk, as in the case of fire-insurance, protects the holder against loss in the event of a fall in the particular piece of property upon which he holds a mortgage, or even in a particular locality. It can not be said, however, that the records are yet sufficiently complete to form a conclusion as to what is a safe proportion between capital and surplus and outstanding mortgages. Further than that the guaranteeing companies, generally speaking, have been operating since their inception upon a rising market, so that their success hitherto has not been remarkable. Allowing for these drawbacks, however, the private investor, unless so situated as to give personal attention to the details of his investments, will probably do well to purchase his mortgages in guaranteed form.

V

INDUSTRIAL BONDS

Industrial bonds include the obligations of all manufacturing and mercantile companies, and miscellaneous companies of a private character. They form a class quite distinct from railroad bonds or public-utility bonds.

I. *Safety of Principal and Interest.* The safety of industrial bonds, in common with the safety of all forms of investment, depends upon the margin of security in excess of the amount of the obligation. In the case of industrial bonds the amount of this margin is not always easy to determine. Even when determined, the rule is difficult of application because a margin which may seem insufficient from the point of view of physical valuation may be satisfactory when considered as the equity of a working concern. The indications most to be relied upon in estimating the safety of industrial bonds are as follows:

(*a*) *Value of real estate.* The first point to be determined in considering the purchase of an industrial bond is the value of the real estate upon which it is a first mortgage. If the appraised value of the ground, irrespective of the buildings and machinery upon it, is greater by a substantial sum than the amount of the bond issue, the obligation is practically a real-estate mortgage. In such a case, while possibly "slow," *i.e.*, secured by an assets difficult to realize upon—the safety of the bond can hardly be questioned. In judging a bond upon its real-estate value, it is not always safe to take the cost price of the land as shown by the company's books, because frequently the cost upon the books is artificially raised by payment having been made in securities whose market value is less than par, or in other ways. As stated above, judgment should be based upon the *appraised* value of the land.

If the bond meets this test satisfactorily, the prospective investor may feel reasonably sure that the safety of his principal is not in question, and may buy the bond without anxiety if it satisfies his other requirements. On the other hand, if the bond only partially meets this test, and it appears that some part of its value comes from plant and equipment and from the strength of the company as a working concern, then it is necessary for the investor to consider carefully several other factors.

(*b*) *Net quick assets.* The balance-sheet of every industrial company can be divided horizontally into two parts. Its assets are of two kinds—property assets, which are fixt, and current assets, which are fluid. Similarly, its liabilities are of two kinds—capital liabilities and current liabilities. It requires no very extended business experience to pick out the items which make up these totals. Plant and property assets are usually lumped together under the head, "Cost of Property." Current assets include inventories, bills and accounts receivable, agents' balances, marketable securities, and cash on hand and in banks—everything, in short, which can be quickly converted into cash. On the other side of the balance-sheet, capital liabilities are easily determined. They consist of the par amounts of bonds and stocks outstanding. Current liabilities comprise bills and accounts payable, including borrowed money, pay-rolls, and interest and taxes accrued but not due.

The real strength of every industrial concern is to be learned from the figures relating to its current accounts. Property assets and capital liabilities are not of the same significance. If the cost of plant and equipment as shown by the books exceeds its real value, the market usually makes the necessary adjustment by putting a price less than par upon the bonds and stocks.

No such process is possible in the case of the current accounts. If the current liabilities exceed the current assets the company shows a deficit, whatever its surplus may show on the books. On the other hand, if the current assets are greater than the current liabilities, the company possesses a working capital, represented by the difference between the two, and known as net quick assets.

There are three things to consider in connection with net quick assets: First, the proportion between current assets and current liabilities. To put a company in good shape its current assets should be at least twice as great as its current liabilities. Two for one is a fair proportion, tho some companies show as much as six to one. The stronger a company is in this proportion the better.

Secondly, the proportion between net quick assets and bonded debt. The bonded debt should never exceed net quick assets, except when the company possesses real estate, in which case two-thirds of the real-estate value plus the net quick assets should cover the bonds. Some companies do much better than that. One prominent company in this country, altho it possesses real estate of considerable value, has agreed in the indenture securing its bonds to keep net quick assets at all times greater by a substantial margin than the amount of bonds outstanding.

Thirdly, the proportion between net quick assets and the surplus as shown in the balance-sheet. If the capital liabilities exactly balance the property assets, it is plain that the surplus will exactly balance the net quick assets. If the surplus is smaller than net quick assets, it is usually a sign that capital liabilities have been created to provide working capital. Opinions differ as to the wisdom of this course. Generally speaking, it is better to provide working capital by means of a stock issue than to depend upon the banks for accommodation. The exception to this rule occurs in the case of companies that require a great deal of working capital for part of the year and only a little at other times. If they have the best banking connections, such companies may be safe in depending upon their banks to carry them, but if they do so, they should have no bonded or other fixt indebtedness which would prevent their paper from being a first lien upon their entire assets.

If working capital is to be created by the issue of capital liabilities, it is much better that it should be done by stocks than by bonds. The ideal method, however, is to provide only such an amount of working capital at the organization of a company as is necessary for the conduct of its business, and then, as the volume of its business grows, to accumulate the additional amount necessary out of earnings, refraining from the payment of dividends until the fund is complete.

Before leaving the subject of net quick assets, it is well to note the importance of the figure showing the actual amount of current liabilities. If a company has outstanding large amounts of bills and notes payable, it occupies a vulnerable position. Inability to renew maturing notes was the cause of most of the industrial failures of last year.

(*c*) *Net Earnings.* The amount of net earnings is of great importance in estimating the strength of an industrial company. The figures for a number of years should be examined to determine whether the earnings are increasing or decreasing, and to discover whether or not the earning power of the company is stable. This will depend largely upon the nature of the article which the company produces or trades in. If its product enjoys a steady demand at a fairly uniform price, it is justifiable that some of its capital should be in the form of bonds; but if its earnings are subject to violent fluctuations due to rapid changes in the price of its product, there is little justification for conducting the business on borrowed money.

In this connection it should always be considered how greatly a falling off in gross earnings will affect net earnings; and the proportion between net earnings and fixt charges should be carefully noted.

In order for an industrial bond to receive favorable consideration, the average yearly net earnings of the company should amount to about three times the annual bond interest, taxes, and sinking funds. The greater the protection is in this respect the better.

(*d*) *Form of Issue.* The form in which an industrial bond is issued is a matter of some importance. If the principal of the bond does not become due for a number of years, there is danger that the property will depreciate so far in value as to leave the bond without sufficient margin of protection. There are two ways to overcome this difficulty. One way is to establish a sinking-fund which will retire a certain proportion of the bonds by lot each year. Another way is to issue the bonds in serial form, with a definite instalment maturing every year. In either case the annual sinking-fund or annual instalment should be greater than the probable depreciation so that the margin of security will be constantly increasing.

(*e*) *Management and Control.* No question is of greater importance in estimating the strength of an industrial company than the reputation of the men in charge. The ability and integrity of the men who control the policy of the company and the efficiency of the operating officials are the principal factors in the success of an industrial undertaking. Vacillating policies, weakly executed, will ruin the most promising enterprise. This is particularly true in the case of small companies. Every man of business experience will understand the importance of this factor and be guided by it in the selection of industrial securities.

Based upon the foregoing considerations it is of interest to inquire what degree of safety really attaches to the average industrial bond? How far does it meet the foregoing requirements? The question is difficult to answer. Industrial bonds vary greatly in point of safety, some issues possessing great strength and others being highly speculative. No general conclusions can be depended upon, and the investor is forced to consider each issue upon its own merits.

II. *Rate of Income.* The average net return upon industrial bonds is probably higher than upon any other form of funded corporate obligation. This constitutes one of the chief advantages of industrial bonds.

III. *Convertibility.* It is impossible to make any general statement in regard to the convertibility of industrial bonds. Some industrial bonds, notably the larger issues of well-known trusts, command a broad and active market. Such bonds can be sold in large amounts at almost any time without seriously affecting the price. On the other hand, small underlying issues of such companies, usually high-grade in point of security, or the obligations of smaller companies, are almost as unmarketable as real-estate mortgages. Between these two extremes all varieties of industrial bonds are to be found. The degree of convertibility which a security possesses is usually a matter of some importance, and the investor should make a careful examination of each bond in this respect.

IV. *Prospect of Appreciation in Value.* To what extent a bond may improve in security during the time that an investor holds it is of little importance unless the improvement be reflected in the market price of the bond. Only so can the investor take advantage of its appreciation in value. In order for the improvement in security to be reflected in market price and thus add to the principal invested, it is necessary that a bond should possess a fairly active market. For this reason the industrial bonds which hold out the greatest promise of appreciation in value are the larger, more speculative issues, which possess the greatest convertibility. The purchase of such bonds frequently results in substantial profits.

V. *Stability of Market Price.* The four points above touched upon—safety, rate of income, convertibility, and likelihood of improvement in intrinsic value—are all inherent characteristics of every bond. The likelihood of favorable or unfavorable fluctuation in market price is largely external in its nature and depends upon general financial and business conditions.

As a class, industrial bonds can not be said to possess much stability of market price. Some of the smaller issues enjoy a fictitious stability because of their inactivity, but generally speaking industrial bonds are subject to wide fluctuations in accordance with changes in the business outlook.

The foregoing is a summary, necessarily brief and imperfect, of the main points to be considered in judging the value of industrial bonds. The question remains whether such securities are desirable for the investment of a business surplus and of private funds.

Except in special cases industrial bonds are not suitable for a business surplus. It is impossible to find an industrial bond which combines all the characteristics necessary for that purpose. The requirements are great safety of principal and interest, a relatively high return, ready convertibility, and stability of market price. Many industrial bonds can be found which combine two of these requirements, some even which combine three, but the full combination, if it exists at all, is unknown to the writer.

In addition, the principle of distribution of risk should prevent one industrial company from investing its reserve funds in the securities of another industrial company.

For private investment the case is somewhat different. A man of good business judgment, who desires to obtain a high yield for which he is prepared to sacrifice something in the way of convertibility and prospect of appreciation in value, may buy the underlying issues of strong companies with every confidence in the safety of his principal. Again, the investor who wants a high yield and quick convertibility, who is prepared to take a business man's risk and to sacrifice stability of market price, may make a large profit by buying second-grade industrial bonds. No investor, however, should deceive himself with the idea that any industrial bond will satisfy all the requirements of the ideal investment.

VI

PUBLIC-UTILITY BONDS

It was a common saying among bond-dealers a few years ago that the day of the municipal bond had passed, the day of the railroad bond was passing, and the day of the public-utility bond was to be. Municipal bonds were selling at fancy prices in consequence of the low rates for money which then prevailed, and railroad bonds appeared to be following in their wake. Public-utility bonds alone afforded a satisfactory yield, and it was felt that the investing public would be forced to turn to them.

This prediction, like many others which were based upon the assumption of continued ease in money, was destined to be unfulfilled. Almost immediately there appeared an added demand for capital, and in the face of this demand, supplies of capital which had before seemed ample became suddenly scarce. Money rates rose rapidly and as a necessary consequence municipal and railroad bonds fell in price to a point where their net return was commensurate with that obtained from the loaning of free capital. The investment situation was thus completely reversed. It was no longer a question as to what form of security investors must seek in order to obtain a satisfactory yield, but rather could the highest grade of municipal and railroad bonds be floated at any price. Under these circumstances the contemplated necessity of turning to public-utility bonds never arose, and the general investing public remains for the most part unfamiliar with their elements of strength and of weakness.

The term "public-utility company" denotes a private corporation supplying public needs under authority of a public franchise. The franchise may be of definite date or perpetual, and may be partial or exclusive.

Public-utility companies include street-railway, gas, electric-light and power, and water companies. Properly speaking, telephone companies should also be included, but they are not usually regarded as belonging to the class of public-service corporations.

It is impossible, within the limits of a single chapter, to discuss each kind of company separately. The investment value of street-railway bonds will be here considered, and it is felt that the general principles advanced, with slight modifications of detail, will be found equally applicable to a judgment of other forms of public-service securities.

I. *Safety of Principal and Interest.* In order to determine the safety of a street-railway company's bonds, the company must be subjected to a threefold examination, physical, financial, and political.

An examination must be made into the extent and condition of the physical property in order to ascertain whether the bonded debt is secured by property having a real market value in excess of the face amount of bonds issued. The first point to be determined is the extent and valuation of the company's real estate. If the appraised value of the land upon which power-houses and car-barns have been erected is alone greater than the amount of bonds outstanding, the investigation need go no further, for the bonds, in such a case, would be practically a real-estate mortgage. In most instances, however, this is very far from being the case; and after careful appraisal of the real estate it is then necessary to make a careful valuation of the other physical property; namely, power-plants, depots, car-sheds, roadway, and equipment.

It is usually impossible for the average investor to make such an examination himself, nor is it likely that he would possess sufficient technical knowledge to render his investigation of much value. For an accurate estimate of the value of a street-railway's physical property, it is usually necessary to depend upon the expert opinion of a trained engineer. It is a matter of regret that the average street-railway report can not be relied upon to furnish an accurate valuation of the physical property; and it is accordingly customary for careful bond-dealers, when they contemplate taking an issue of street-railway bonds for distribution among their clients, to have the property examined by a competent engineer, whose report then determines for them the question of taking the issue.

Disregarding the figures which show the cost of property and equipment upon the company's books, the engineer proceeds to make a careful estimate of the replacement value of the property, including real estate. If the result of the examination shows that the property could not be duplicated for the amount of the bond issue, the company occupies an unusually strong position—altho even in such a case some part of the value of the bonds comes from the strength of the company as a going concern.

In most cases, however, it is probably found that the bond issue is in excess of the value of real estate and the replacement value of the physical property, the balance representing a capitalization of the franchise.

To determine the real value of the franchise or franchises is a difficult matter and involves the whole question of the company's relations with the community which it serves and with the local lawmaking bodies.

The first question which arises is whether the franchise is perpetual or for a definite time, and the second whether it is partial or exclusive. Franchises vary greatly in these respects. Sometimes a franchise, apparently partial, is practically exclusive, owing to the fact that all the available space in the streets is already occupied by the company's own tracks. If the franchises of a company are limited as to time, it is expedient, if not imperative, that the bonds should mature before the expiration of the franchises.

If the company whose bonds are under examination satisfactorily passes this physical test—if it possesses real estate of considerable value, if the replacement value of the property is as great or nearly as great as the amount of the bonds, and if the franchises, while perhaps not perpetual or exclusive, are yet of longer duration than the bonds and render successful competition unlikely—the next step may then be taken; that is to say, an examination of the company's financial condition and earning capacity may be made.

The amount of its gross earnings should be examined and the figures scrutinized for a number of years back to discover whether its earnings are increasing or decreasing. The position in which the company stands for obtaining new traffic must be noted, and some estimate must be made of the stability of its earning power. In this connection the relations of the company to the public are of great importance. It must be learned whether the company follows the policy of conciliating or ignoring public sentiment.

The net earnings of the company must then be examined. This involves a criticism of operating expenses. The payments of the road must be analyzed to determine whether the proper amounts have been expended for renewal of track, replenishment of rolling stock, and other improvement sufficient to keep the property in good physical condition. This is the most intricate subject in the investigation of a street-railway property. Unless proper allowance be made for depreciation, in addition to the expenses of direct operation, it is only a question of time before the strongest company will become bankrupt.

Deterioration of plant and equipment, which goes on constantly, can only be offset in two ways: one is out of earnings and the other is out of the security-holders—that is, by decreases in the market value of the securities. The first takes prosperity or courage; the second leads to bankruptcy. It is difficult to measure depreciation accurately, but a safe rule is to write off ten per cent of gross earnings each month for depreciation. In this way the charge for depreciation will be proportionate to the traffic, which provides automatic adjustment.

If the net earnings, after making this allowance for depreciation, and after providing all expenses of operation including ordinary repairs, amount to as much as twice the interest charges upon the bonds outstanding, it is probable that the bonds may be taken with safety.

Before finally determining the question, however, certain political factors must be taken into consideration. The relations of the company to the leaders of the dominant political party must be investigated. The likelihood of agitation looking toward a reduction of fares must be considered and the possibility of increase in taxes (if below the legal limit) must be weighed. The probable attitude of the legislature on the question of renewing the franchises when they expire must be considered. In general, it must be learned whether any real ground of contention exists between the company on the one hand and the public and its representatives on the other, because it is inevitable that the company will weaken its independence of position by too close a connection with politics, and that the physical property will suffer if there is any lack of uninterrupted attention to it.

Finally one other thing should be investigated—the amount of the accident account and its proportion to the net earnings of the company. On small lines a single case of heavy damages will sometimes make serious inroads upon the earnings.

The foregoing is a summary, necessarily brief and imperfect, but true in its essential outlines, of the main points which should be considered in judging the safety of street-railway bonds. The question remains, how far does the average street-railway company satisfy these requirements? Broadly speaking, street-railway bonds are not yet to be classed in the first rank of investment securities. The troubles which have come to a head in the financial operations of the traction systems in New York and Chicago are typical of troubles which are likely to occur elsewhere from the same general causes—overcapitalization in the first place and insufficient allowance for depreciation in the second place. In both New York and Chicago the crisis was hastened by open and obvious overcapitalization, which is almost inevitable when many independent lines are merged into one system. The same trouble, however, is apt to occur in other traction systems where this evil appeared less flagrant at the outset.

The advantages of electricity over horsepower naturally led to the multiplication of electric street lines, as the system ten or fifteen years ago passed beyond the experimental stage. As in all new enterprises, speculation ran ahead of the reality and financing built upon oversanguine calculations has too often had difficulty in squaring accounts when brought face to face with facts. In most of the calculations insufficient allowance was made for the wear and tear of service; in other words, for renewal of road and equipment. After a few years' test of earnings against expenses, it became evident that a proper allowance for depreciation of plant would show a heavy deficit in the income account. In most cases therefore no allowance or only a meager one was made. For a time this method of bookkeeping proved less disastrous than might have been expected owing to the rapid growth of population and business in American cities. It was possible in many cases to consider the enhanced value given to the franchise by growth of business as an offset to the depreciation of tracks and equipment. In so far also as the plant was kept up to a high degree of efficiency by charging the expense of repairs to operating expenses, the absence of a depreciation account was partially offset.

With the progress of recent years, however, a new factor has been entering into the problem which promises to make the situation still more serious for the traction systems. This new factor is the rise in prices and wages. Temporarily the influence of this factor may be checked by diminished business activity, but when normal conditions are restored, it will commence to act again upon the railways with accumulated effect.

In most cases a proposition to increase the standard street-railway fare above five cents as an offset to the increased operating expenses would be so revolutionary a proposal that it could hardly be carried through. With the line of cost converging upon the line of receipts and with no proper allowance made for depreciation, the traction systems of the country seem to be facing a difficult problem. In the long run it can not be doubted that the problem will be met and solved in a way to afford justice alike to the public who use the cars and to the capitalists who have made street traction on a large scale possible, but in the meantime the investor who desires perfect safety should exercise great care and discrimination in his purchases of street-railway obligations.

II. *Rate of Income.* As a general rule, street-railway bonds in common with the obligations of all public-service corporations sell upon about the same income basis as high-grade industrial bonds—that is to say, under normal conditions they return considerably more than railroad or municipal bonds.

III. *Convertibility.* It is difficult to speak of the convertibility of public-utility bonds as a class for the reason that they differ widely from one another in this respect. In general, it is certainly more difficult to dispose of public-utility bonds than railroad bonds. They do not possess sufficient convertibility to justify their purchase by any one who may need to realize quickly on his holdings.

IV. *Prospect of Appreciation in Value.* Public-utility bonds, except such issues as are convertible into stock, possess little prospect of appreciation in value. It was pointed out above that depreciation is not properly allowed for, and it is very difficult for the securities to advance in the face of this obstacle.

V. *Stability of Market Price.* The bonds of public-service corporations are relatively more stable than railroad bonds because their earnings are not subject to the fluctuations which occur in railroad properties between years of prosperity and years of depression. At the same time, it should be pointed out that their stability of price is largely fictitious, owing to the comparative inactivity of the issues. In other words, while the quotation may be maintained, it is usually difficult to sell any large quantity of a public-service corporation's bonds in a period of financial disturbance, while railroad bonds are more easily liquidated even if at a sacrifice.

The question remains, do public-utility bonds afford a desirable security for the investment of a business surplus and of private funds? In regard to the former, it may be said at once that public-utility bonds do not meet the necessary conditions. The security is too doubtful, the convertibility is too small, and the stability of price too uncertain.

For private investment the case is somewhat different. Keeping in mind the desirability of diversifying investments and admitting the attractiveness of investing in a class of property whose earnings are comparatively stable, it seems clear that public-utility bonds can not be dismissed without consideration. When a company is found whose property is substantially equal in real value to its bonded debt, whose allowance for depreciation is ample, whose franchises are satisfactory, whose earning capacity is large, and whose management is capable and upright, the investor is justified in giving careful consideration to its issues. Unless all these points are found to be satisfactory, however, the investor should content himself with some other form of security. For some years to come it is to be feared that many of our public-service corporations will suffer from the war of discordant elements—disregard of the rights of the public on the part of the management and socialistic agitation for control on the part of the community. Until these warring factions are reconciled and the questions at issue adjusted with fairness to the security-holders and the public, the investor should be most prudent in his purchases of public-utility obligations.

VII

MUNICIPAL BONDS

The previous chapters have considered, in turn, the investment value of railroad bonds, real-estate mortgages, industrial bonds, and public-utility bonds. The desirability of each of these different classes of security has been judged in accordance with the general principles laid down in the introductory chapter; that is to say, each class has been analyzed in relation to safety, rate of income, convertibility, prospect of appreciation in value and stability of market price. The same determining factors must now be applied to a judgment of government, State, and municipal bonds.

Bonds issued by a national government, by a State, or by a municipality are based primarily on some form of the power of taxation, tho the bonds are usually tax exempt within the political unit which creates them.

When the power of taxation is unlimited, as in the case of the national government and the sovereign States, there can be no question as to the ability of the political unit to meet its obligation, and the question becomes entirely one of good faith. It is probable that the obligations of the United States Government, by reason of the fact that the per-capita debt of the country is so small, the wealth of the country so great, and the good faith of the American people so clearly established, represent the highest type of security to be found in the world. It is quite possible, therefore, that the 2-per-cent United States Consols would sell in any case at a relatively higher price than the obligations of any other country, but it can not be denied that the chief reason which causes them to sell at the remarkably high price which they have attained is the fact that they are required by national banks as security for circulation. This fact is doubtless the controlling element in their market position, and at once accounts for their special strength and removes them from the field of private investment.

Only less secure than United States bonds are the obligations of the sovereign States of the Union. State bonds usually sell upon a basis which may be taken as the equivalent of pure interest, with no element of risk or speculation involved. The obligations of different States sell at different prices, in accordance with market conditions and the relations of supply and demand, but there can be no question of the equal ability of all States to pay their obligations. Repudiation of State debts has occurred in our history, but only in cases where an overwhelming majority of the citizens were opposed to the creation of the debt at the time of its issue, but lacked the means to control the situation. Such instances are chiefly to be found in the case of the so-called carpet-bag governments of the Southern States after the Civil War.

Municipal bonds—*i.e.*, the bonds of cities, counties, and townships—are indirectly a first lien upon all taxable property in the municipality, and take precedence of every form of mortgage or judgment lien. This lien is enforced through a tax levy to meet interest and principal, and this tax levy the courts will compel in the rare cases in which a municipality attempts to repudiate a valid bond. This priority of the tax lien is the foundation of the prime position of municipal bonds. The case rarely occurs where a bond held valid by the courts proves uncollectable if sufficient taxing power existed when the bond was issued to provide for its redemption. It is only when the municipality itself diminishes in population and taxable property to the vanishing-point that such a default can occur. An investor can judge for himself as to the likelihood of such a catastrophe in any particular community, and can feel sure that his bond, if valid and protected by a sufficient taxing power, is as secure in its principal and interest as the municipality which issues it is secure in its continued existence. The following are the chief points which should be considered in the investigation of a municipal bond: (1) The proportion which the total debt of the municipality bears to the assessed valuation of the property subject to taxation. Usually a maximum rate is fixt by constitutional provision which rarely exceeds 10 per cent. (2) The purpose of issue. This must be a proper and suitable one. (3) The proceedings under which the bonds were issued. These proceedings, the form of bonds, their execution, and their legal details must be in full compliance with the law.

If these points are found to be satisfactory, the investor may rest content that no other form of security is so greatly safeguarded and that his bond ranks upon a substantial equality with government and State obligations.

The rate of income to be derived from investment in municipal bonds varies in accordance with the obligations selected. Like other forms of security, municipal bonds are controlled by market conditions, and their price is determined by the relations of supply and demand, and by adjustment to prevailing money rates. While differing only moderately from one another in point of safety and income return, municipal bonds may be divided into two distinct classes in accordance with the degree of convertibility which they possess. Some municipal bonds possess great convertibility; others almost none. The feature which chiefly determines the activity or inactivity of a municipal issue is the size and importance of the municipality, together with the amount of bonds which it has outstanding. The bonds of large and important cities, whose outstanding debt reaches considerable proportions, usually possess great activity. They are constantly traded in and command a broad market because dealers are willing to buy or sell them in blocks at prices within a fraction of 1 per cent apart.

On the other hand, the bonds of counties, townships, and small cities are usually quite inactive. Transactions rarely occur in them, dealers do not make a market in them, and they can be sold only to genuine investors. It is often impossible to have them even quoted.

At first sight, it would appear that active municipal bonds would be much more desirable, but inactive municipals possess a special advantage which the active ones do not enjoy. They possess more stability of market price. It is true that their stability of value is due to the fact that they are not traded in or quoted and is, therefore, largely fictitious, but nevertheless it accomplished a useful purpose. It enables the investor to carry inactive municipals at cost price upon his books through periods in which active market bonds would require to be marked down in conformity with prevailing market prices. No other class of investment except real-estate mortgages possesses to the same degree this quality of price stability. For many classes of buyers—savings-banks, for example—stability of price is a consideration of prime importance. The preservation of the savings-bank's surplus and, indeed, the continued solvency of the institution depend upon maintaining the integrity of the principal which it has invested. A savings-bank requires, also, great safety of principal and interest; *i.e.*, the certainty that principal and interest instalments will be paid at maturity. It needs only a fair but not high yield, and it does not need to place emphasis upon convertibility or prospect of appreciation in value. Comparison of these requirements with the characteristics of inactive municipal bonds discloses a striking adaptability on their part to the real needs of the case. As a consequence, it is not surprizing to discover that inactive municipals are greatly sought by savings-banks.

The desirability of inactive municipals for savings-bank investment was never more forcibly illustrated than on the first of last January, when the savings-banks came to make up their annual statements. Broadly speaking, there can be no doubt that they were saved by the large quantity of inactive municipals and real-estate mortgages which they carried. Had any considerable portion of their assets consisted of railroad bonds and active municipals, upon which they should have had to write off a loss of ten to fifteen points, their solvency would almost certainly have been impaired.

But we are chiefly concerned in these pages with the advantages and disadvantages of different forms of investment from the point of view of a business man, both for the investment of his business surplus and of his private funds. Do municipal bonds, either active or inactive, conform to the requirements of the business surplus? It can not be said that they do. Municipal bonds possess either convertibility without stability of price or stability of price without convertibility. Both qualities are necessary for a business surplus. The only form of municipal security which is at all adapted for the investment of a business surplus is a short-term issue of an active municipal bond. If it has only a very few years to run, its constant approach to maturity will invest it with the necessary stability of price. But even in this case equal safety and equal stability of price combined with a higher yield can probably be found in some high-grade railroad issue— either a short-term mortgage or equipment bond.

For private investment the case is somewhat different. Enough has been said in the preceding chapters to impress upon the reader the importance of buying securities only in accordance with his real requirements. If any investor, after careful comparison of the characteristics of municipal bonds, either active or inactive, with his necessities, decides that he can more closely satisfy his requirements with municipals than with any other form of security, he should not hesitate to purchase them. It is the opinion of the writer, however, that a thorough survey of the field of investment will generally disclose to the investor some security in either the railroad or corporation field which will suit his requirements as well as the municipal bond and at the same time provide him with a greater income.

VIII

STOCKS

Passing to the consideration of stocks as investments, it is necessary at the outset that the reader should have clearly in mind the fundamental difference between stocks and bonds. This distinction was drawn in the introductory chapter, but it will be well to amplify it here, even at the risk of carrying the reader over familiar ground.

The distinction between bonds and stocks is that between *promises to pay* and *equities*. Bonds, loans on collateral, and real-estate mortgages represent some one's promise to pay a sum of money at a future date; and if the promise be valid and the security ample, the holder of the promise will be paid the money on the date due. Stocks, on the other hand, represent only a beneficial interest or residuary share in the assets and profits of a working concern after payment of its obligations and fixt charges. The value of the residuary share may be large or small, may increase or diminish, but in no case can the holder of such a share require any one, least of all the company itself, to take his share off his hands at the price he paid for it, or, indeed, at any price. If a man buys a $1,000 railroad bond, he knows that the railroad, if solvent, will pay him $1,000 in cash when the bond matures, but if he buys a share of railroad stock his only chance of getting his money back, if he should wish it, is that some one else will want to buy his share from him at the price he paid for it or more. If he buys a bond he becomes a creditor of the company, without voice in its management, but entitled to receive his principal and interest when due under pain of forfeiture of the security which the company made over to the trustee to insure payment. If he buys stock, he becomes a partner in a business enterprise, exercising his proportionate share in the direction of the company's affairs, and sharing ratably in its profits and losses. In the one case he buys a promise to pay and in the other an equity.

This distinction, which appears plainly marked in theory, has been much obscured in recent years by the influence of two factors. As the country grew in size, the large corporations—the railroads, for example—required greater capital in order to provide facilities for the handling of their growing business. It was impossible to provide this capital wholly by means of bond issues without destroying the proportion between bonds and stocks, which alone could give to the bondholders the protection of a substantial equity. It was therefore necessary to obtain a large part of the capital required in the form of stock. The railway-managers were thus confronted with a difficult problem. It was imperative that they should obtain more capital, and it was impossible to dispose of sufficient stock on the basis of a speculative risk in a business venture. It was therefore necessary for the railway-managers to emphasize, as far as possible, the investment character of their stock, and various expedients were adopted to accomplish this purpose. In some cases preferred stocks were created or resulted from reorganizations, which possest a first lien upon the assets after payment of the obligations, and which were entitled to a certain stipulated dividend before the common stock obtained any distribution from the earnings. In this way the railway-managers created a compromise security which could be regarded as a stock, and would thus provide equity from the bondholders' point of view, and, at the same time, one which could be disposed of to investors. In other cases, which were probably more numerous, railway-managers attempted to give their stock an investment value through stability of income return. In good years when the company earned 10 or 15 per cent on its stock, their policy was to pay only 5 or 6 per cent in dividends, and hold the rest in their surplus fund in order to have the means of paying the same dividends the next year if only 2 or 3 per cent should be earned. By giving their stock stability of income return they hoped and expected to give it some stability of market price, and thus make it attractive to genuine investors. The effect of this policy was unquestionably successful, and one after another the stocks of our more important transportation systems and other large undertakings passed into the hands of investors.

The successful adoption of this policy on the part of the railway-managers and other captains of industry has had one curious effect which was not contemplated by the originators of the movement, and which brings us to the second influence mentioned above as having tended to obscure the distinction between bonds and stocks. When a case has been brought before the courts in which the contention was advanced that the charges of the railway or public-service corporation were too high, the courts appear to have taken the ground that stocks and bonds should be classed together in order to determine the aggregate capitalization of the company, and that the justice or injustice of the contention that the charges are too high should be determined by ascertaining whether if the charges were made lower the net earnings would still be sufficient to pay a fair return on the total capital invested. This is the general line of reasoning pursued by the courts, both in the case of the Consolidated Gas Company in New York and the Pennsylvania Railroad in Pennsylvania. The effect of this attitude on the part of the courts has been to obscure still more greatly the real distinction between bonds and stocks. It is too early as yet to judge what will be the final outcome of the changed attitude toward stocks, but it can not be doubted that the present tendency of opinion on the subject, so far as large corporations are concerned, is to limit the return on stocks to a strictly investment basis, instead of leaving the stockholders free to reap all possible profit from their business venture subject to the restraints of competition.

The adoption of this attitude by the courts should be a matter for serious consideration on the part of present and prospective stockholders. If the maximum return on stock is to be limited to 6 per cent, or any fair investment basis, and charges reduced to consumers so that they obtain the benefit of any greater earning power, it would appear that the stockholders occupy an undesirable position. With their possible profits limited, but with no fixt return insured to them and no guaranty against possible loss, it can not be held that the purchase of stock seems attractive.

These questions, however, will doubtless be settled in the long run in justice both to the public and to the stockholders, and in the meantime the stocks of our large and successful railway and industrial corporations, which have attained a certain stability and permanence of value, are entitled to consideration when investments are contemplated. It is not worth while to lay down rules for judging the investment value of such stocks, because the general principles advanced in the preceding chapters will be found sufficient for a judgment of their values.

One class of stocks, however, deserves special mention. Bank and trust-company stocks possess one characteristic in higher degree than other classes of stock. Owing to the general practise of self-regulated banking institutions to distribute only about one-half their earnings in dividends and to credit the rest to surplus account, a steady rise is assured in the book value of the stock. No other class of stock possesses quite the same promise of appreciation in value. Bank and trust-company stocks are especially sought by wealthy men, who can forego something in the way of income return for the sake of increasing the amount of their principal. The general characteristics of bank stocks are great safety, a low rate of income, limited convertibility, and practical certainty of appreciation in value.

With the present chapter the discussion of specific forms of investments has come to an end. The next and concluding chapter will explain the general principles which control the market movements of all negotiable securities, and will endeavor to point out the indications which may be relied upon in determining whether or not given conditions are favorable for the purchase of securities.

IX

MARKET MOVEMENTS OF SECURITIES

There is no question connected with the investment of money more important than the ability to judge whether general market conditions are favorable for the purchase of securities.

After learning how to judge the value of every form of investment, a man may still be unsuccessful in the investment of money unless he acquires also a firm grasp upon the general principles which control the price movements of securities. By this it is not meant that a man needs to have an intimate knowledge of technical market conditions whereby to estimate temporary fluctations of minor importance, but rather that he should have clearly in mind the causes which operate to produce the larger swings of prices. If an investor acquires such a knowledge, he is enabled to take advantage of large price movements in such a way as materially to increase his income, and, at the same time, avoid carrying upon his books securities which may have cost much more than their current market quotations. If he can recognize the indications which point to the beginning of a pronounced upward swing in securities, and if he can equally recognize the signs which indicate that the movement has culminated, he can liquidate the securities which he bought at the inception of the rise or transfer them to some short-term issues whose near approach to maturity will render them stable in price, allowing the downward swing to proceed without disturbing him. It is not expected, of course, that the average business man will be able to realize completely this ideal of investment, but it is hoped that the following analysis will give him a clearer conception of the principles involved.

Broadly speaking, the market movements of all negotiable securities are controlled by two influences, sometimes acting in opposition to each other and sometimes in concert. One of these influences is the loaning rate of free capital; the other is the general condition of business. A low rate of interest or the likelihood of low rates has the effect of stimulating security prices, because banks and other money-lending institutions are forced into the investment market when they can not loan money to advantage. Conversely, a high rate of interest or the prospect of high rates has the effect of depressing prices, because banking institutions sell their securities in order to lend the money so released. The automatic working of this process tends to produce a constant adjustment between the yields upon free and invested capital. When money rates are low, securities tend to advance to the point where the return upon them is no greater than that derived from the loaning of free capital. When rates are high, securities tend to decline to a point where the return is as great. This explains the influence of the first factor.

The other factor is the general condition of business. Good business conditions, or the promise of good conditions, tend to advance security prices, because they indicate larger earnings and a stronger financial condition. Poor business conditions, or an unpromising outlook, have the reverse effect.

The larger movements of security prices are always the resultant of the interaction of these two forces. When they work together the effect is irresistible, as when low interest rates and the prospect of good business conditions occur together, or when high money rates occur in the face of an indicated falling off in business activity. At such times all classes of securities swing together. For the most part, however, money rates and business conditions are opposed in their influence, rates being low when business is bad and high when business is good. Usually the worse business conditions become, the easier money grows; while the more active business becomes, the higher money rates rise. The effect of this antagonism between the controlling causes is to produce movements of different proportions and sometimes in different directions in different classes of securities. High-grade bonds may be declining, middle-grade bonds remaining stationary, and poor bonds advancing, all at the same time. This serves to give a very irregular appearance to the security markets, and appears to justify the widely held opinion that security prices are a pure matter of guesswork, and that they are controlled only by manipulation and special influences. A clear conception of the nature of the influences which are always silently at work reconciles these apparent inconsistencies and makes it plain that general price movements are determined by laws as certain in their operation as the laws of nature.

This may be illustrated by a single example. Let us assume that interest rates are low and business conditions bad with prospect of still lower interest rates and still more unpromising business conditions. What will be the effect upon different classes of securities? High-grade bonds, such as choice municipals, whose safety can not be impaired by any extent of depression in business, will advance because their market price is influenced almost wholly by money rates. If their interest is certain to be paid, no matter what business conditions may become, they can not be greatly affected by a reduction of earnings, and consequently the influence of low money rates is left to act practically alone. Middle-grade bonds, such as second-class railroad issues, will remain almost stationary, low money rates tending to advance their price and the fear of decreased earnings tending to depress them. The lowest grade of bonds and stocks, whose margin of security even in good times is not very great, will probably suffer in price because the fear of default in interest and of reduction in dividends will operate much more strongly than the mere stimulus of low interest rates. Of course, securities can not be clearly separated into these three classes, but shade imperceptibly into one another. The classification is adopted only for purposes of illustration.

Up to this point we have been concerned merely in showing that the market movements of negotiable securities are controlled by the influence of certain factors. A more important question now remains to be considered, viz.: whether the effect of these two influences is to produce general swings in prices which may be depended upon with comparative certainty, and, if so, what indications are afforded to the investor of the commencement or culmination of such a movement. The answer must be that the combined effect of the two influences described is to produce definite and regular swings in prices, and that the indications which define the movements are not difficult to follow.

A general survey of the history of every industrial nation reveals the fact that business conditions undergo alternate periods of prosperity and depression extending in clearly defined cycles of substantially uniform length. By tracing the usual course of interest rates and of business conditions throughout one of these cycles, a general idea can be formed of the way in which the joint influences operate to produce price movements. To what extent the course of interest rates is a cause as well as a result of changing business conditions, we shall not attempt here to estimate, but will be content to note carefully the general course which rates for money pursue throughout the cycles. Immediately after a financial crisis, which usually closes an era of great business prosperity, money rates become abnormally easy. Within a few months from the climax of the crisis, money accumulates in enormous volume in financial centers. This is caused by the great diminution of business activity which renders unnecessary a large part of the circulating medium that was formerly required to transact the greater volume of business. To the extent to which this accumulation of money merely reflects a redundancy of currency as distinguished from real liquid capital, it can have little effect in encouraging the resumption of business activity. As time passes, however, and economies in operation commence to make themselves manifest, and especially as waste and extravagance are curtailed, the country as a whole commences to accumulate real liquid capital; that is to say, its total production leaves a surplus over the amount of consumption. In the state of business feeling which has been pictured, the undertaking of new business ventures or additions to existing properties would not be approved, so that the surplus wealth created finds its way into bank deposits as liquid capital. The competitive attempt to loan this capital at a time when borrowers are few produces merely nominal interest rates. This continues for some time. It is only gradually as confidence returns and as the spirit of initiative begins to reassert itself that some part of the liquid capital created each year is diverted into fixt forms. Here and there some enterprising group of men will develop a mine, lay a new piece of railway, or make some addition to an existing undertaking. For some length of time, however, the liquid capital of the country not only remains unimpaired, but is continually increasing. After a time a change comes. The annual surplus of production, tho larger than before, is only sufficient to provide for the new undertakings which the growing optimism demands. Interest rates rise moderately in response to the added demand for capital. A few years further along, as business activity increases and success appears plainly to wait upon new ventures, the demand for new capital with which to develop increased facilities and new enterprises exceeds the annual supply of wealth created. Prosperity having increased, another factor commences to assert itself. The spirit of economy and thrift which had prevailed throughout the years of depression gives place to extravagance, the demand for luxuries, and other unproductive forms of expenditure. While the total production is much greater than in the lean years, the margin of production is not proportionately as great, and this amount is insufficient to meet the demands upon it. The supplies of liquid capital stored up during the years of depression are resorted to, and they serve to provide the new capital for a few additional years. Interest rates at once reflect the encroachment upon stored-up capital, and their rise gives the first real warning of the country's true position. The optimistic business men do not heed the warning. After exhausting all the real capital available in the country, they proceed to borrow extensively from foreigners or from government banks—in this country from the national government through bank deposits. Every step which can be taken to induce foreigners to part with their capital is resorted to. If foreigners will not buy long-term bonds, short-term notes are created. If the foreigners refuse these, they are asked to make loans secured by the new bonds and notes. The rates of interest offered are so attractive that considerable sums are usually obtained, and the pressure of business activity continues further. Finally the day of reckoning arrives when some incident, usually unimportant in itself, first suggests to the lenders of money that their debtors whom they know to be overextended may not be able to pay their loans. The attempt to collect their loans produces a financial crisis which brings to an end the period of prosperity.

The foregoing is a description of the more important stages through which business conditions pass from crisis to crisis. Different cycles vary in particular details, but all agree in essential outlines. Sometimes special influences are at work which operate to shorten or prolong the cycle. The approach of a crisis will be retarded by inflation of the currency, for the excess finds its way into bank vaults and increases the volume of loanable credit. The effect of such inflation, however, is wholly disastrous, because the addition to the supply of capital is fictitious, not real, and only defers the day of reckoning for a greater catastrophe. On the other hand, the approach of a crisis can be greatly hastened by wars, conflagrations, and other agencies which destroy capital, and by attacks upon capital and the conduct of corporate business, for such attacks tend to render capital timid and produce the same effect as a violent curtailment of the supply. These are only some of the many influences which might become operative, but they serve to show the necessity for careful consideration of all the factors at work if a true conception of the condition and tendencies of business is to be formed.

From the general account given above of the successive phases of a credit cycle, it is possible to summarize the course of interest rates and the course of business conditions. Money rates become suddenly easy after a crisis, remain low or grow easier for a period of several years, and then rise continuously until the next crisis, advancing with great rapidity toward the close of the cycle. Business conditions remain poor or grow worse a few years after a crisis. Liquidation is taking place, prices are going down, and the uncertainty of the outlook causes diminished activity. Thereafter, however, conditions improve and activity increases with fair uniformity until it reaches the high tension of the period immediately preceding the crisis. The course of interest rates and the course of business conditions may both be deflected by the operation of special influences, but the general tendencies are substantially as outlined. The result of the operation of these joint factors may be traced in the market movements of any class of security desired. For the sake of simplicity, let us consider their effect in producing the market swings of the highest grade of investment issues and of the lowest grade, those which are affected only by money rates and those which are affected almost wholly by business conditions.

Emerging from the strain of the crisis at their lowest point, high-grade bonds, such as the best municipal and railroad issues, advance rapidly as interest rates decline, continuing their advancing tendency throughout the period of business depression which follows upon the heels of the crisis. As business conditions improve, their position, while perfectly secure before, is further strengthened and an added stimulus is given to their rise. About the middle of the cycle when the business outlook is very promising, and before interest rates have sustained any material advance, the prices of high-grade bonds are usually at their highest point. From that time forward they commence to decline, in spite of the increasing prosperity of the country, under the influence of rising money rates. They make their lowest prices in the midst of the crisis, when the strain upon capital is greatest and the outlook for business most unpromising.

The lowest grade of bonds, on the other hand (whose margin of security is least), do not commence to recover materially in price, in spite of the influence of low money rates during the hard times which follow the crisis, the influence of reduced earnings and the fear of default of interest holding them in check. As the outlook becomes brighter, they advance rapidly and continue to improve in price so long as they yield more than current money rates. At some point, difficult to determine in advance but usually well along toward the end of the cycle, they reach their high point and thereafter decline under the influence of the growing stringency in money.

Between these two extremes, every class of security is to be found. The better ones will tend to resemble, in their market movements, the course pursued by the choicest bonds; the poorer ones will approximate the lowest class. In every case, however, unless special influences operate to produce variations, the market swing of a given security should be easily conjectured by an investor who gives careful attention to the relative weight which is likely to attach to each determining influence.

www.ingramcontent.com/pod-product-compliance
Lightning Source LLC
Chambersburg PA
CBHW081246220326
41597CB00024BB/4434